Mignon Manhart

This book will tell you about some fantastic fish.
For each fish you will also find:

a photo of it

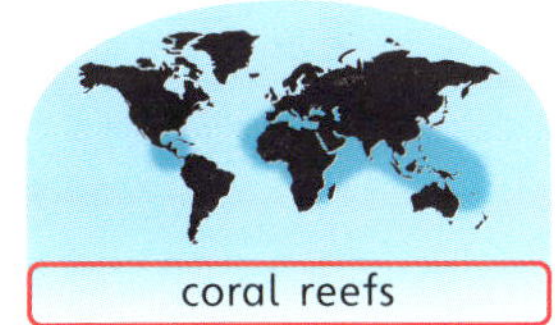

a map to show where it lives

a scale to show its size

Angler Fish

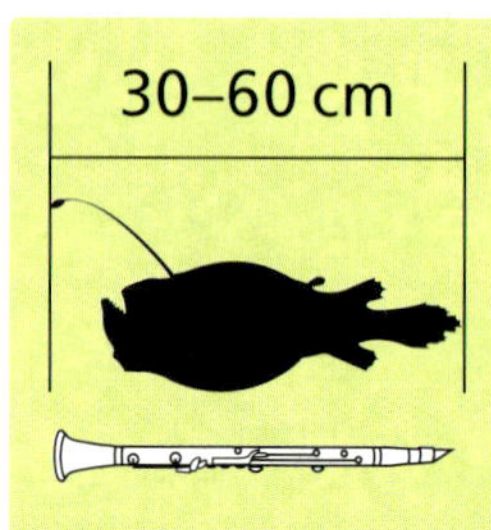

The deep-sea angler fish uses a rod to fish for its dinner.

It is very dark in deep waters, so the angler fish has a light at the tip of its rod. When other fish see the light, they come close. Then the angler fish catches them!

light

Blind Catfish

Blind catfish live in dark caves. They have eyes, but they can't see. They use their whiskers to find food and to feel where they are going.

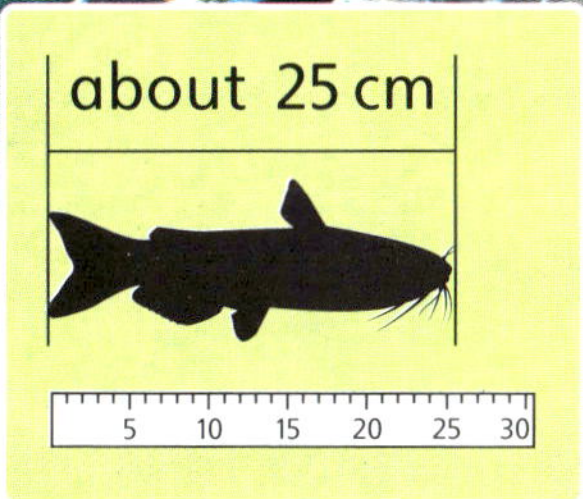

whiskers

about 25 cm

5 10 15 20 25 30

Clown Fish

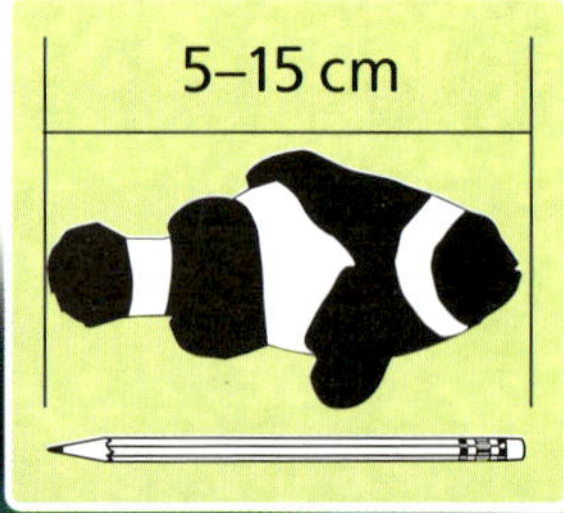

5–15 cm

Clown fish live between the **tentacles** of **sea anemones**. The tentacles contain poison, which protects the clown fish from **predators**.

coral reefs

Dwarf Goby

0.5 cm

The dwarf goby is the size of a ladybird. It is the smallest fish in the world.

Electric Eel

An electric eel makes its own electricity. It stuns nearby fish and frogs with an electric shock from its tail. Then it eats them.

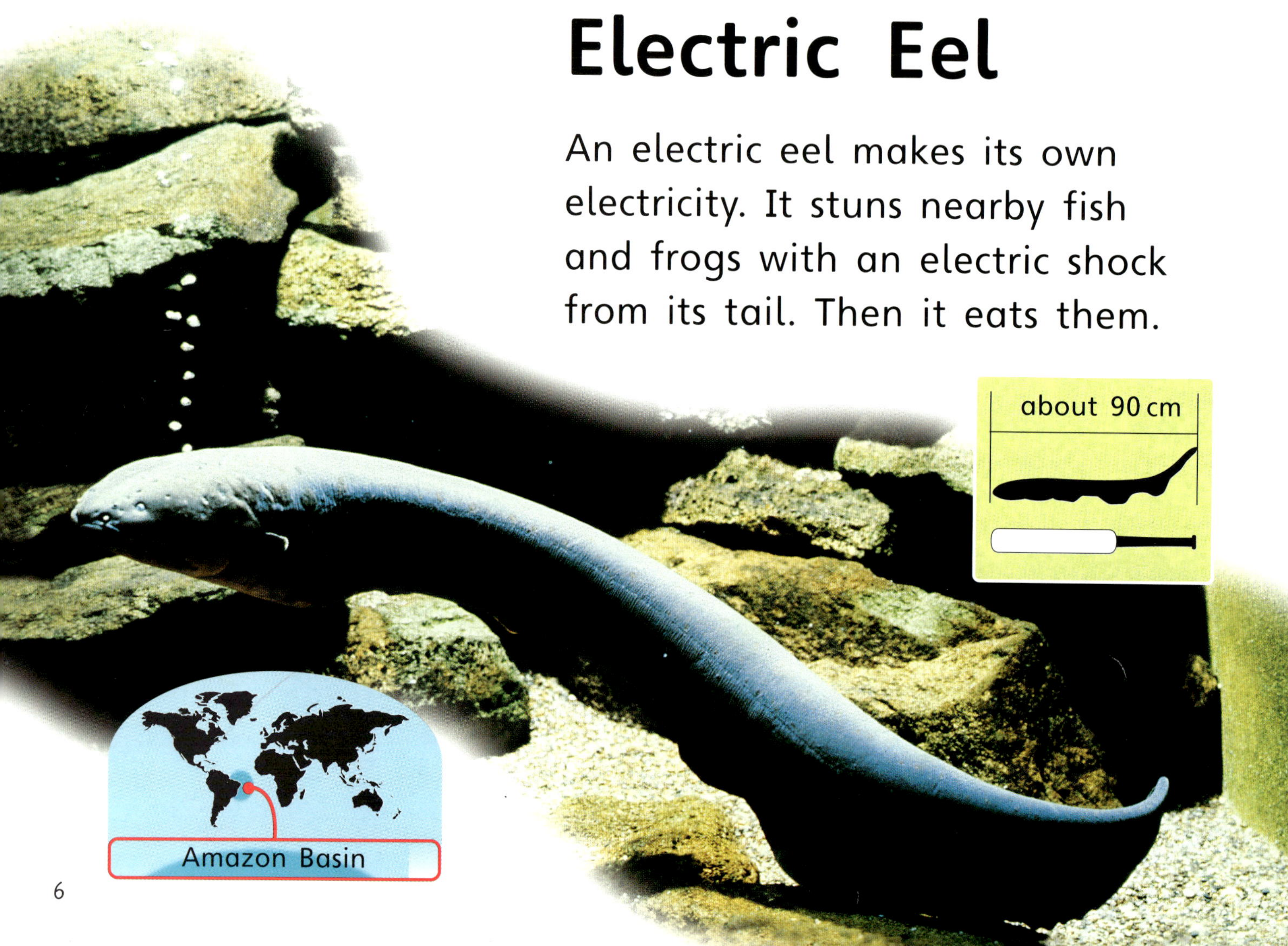

Frog Fish

about 12.5cm

Frog fish live among the rocks on the bottom of the warmer seas. Instead of swimming, they use their fins to hop along.

warm seas

Grunt

A grunt grinds its teeth, making a sound like a pig. Two grunts may swim with their red mouths together. That is why they are also called kissing fish.

tropical seas

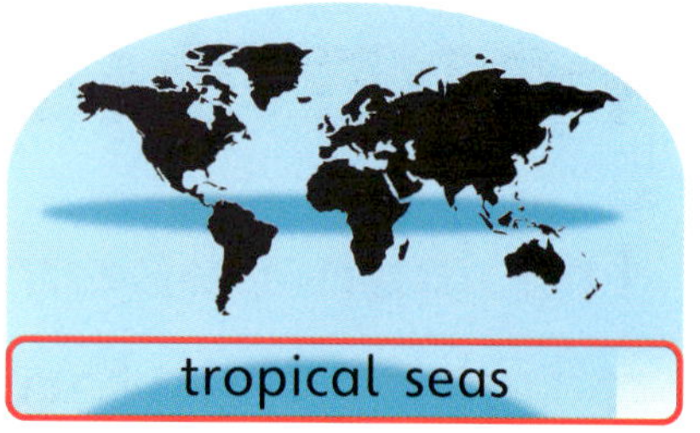

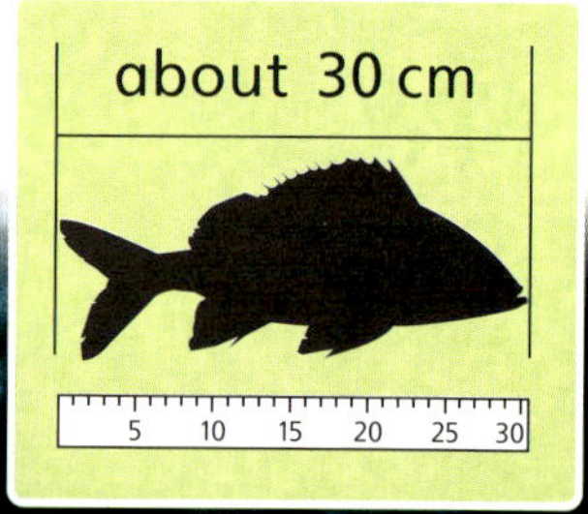

about 30 cm
5 10 15 20 25 30

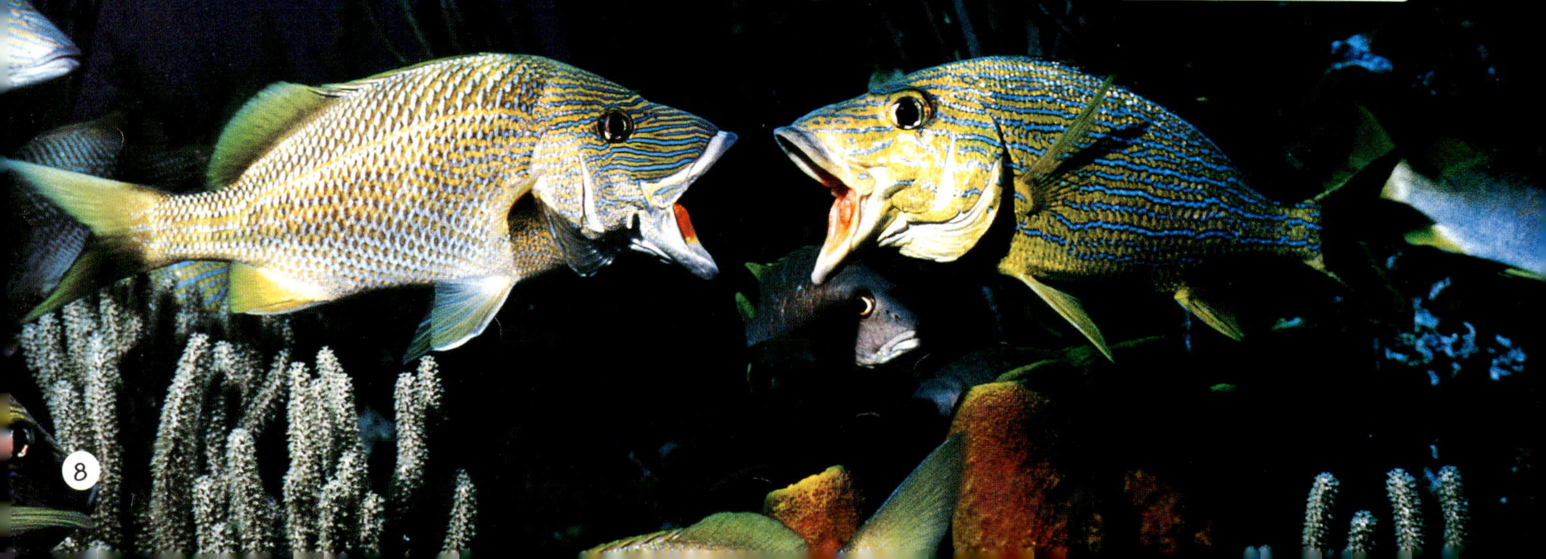

Hammerhead Shark

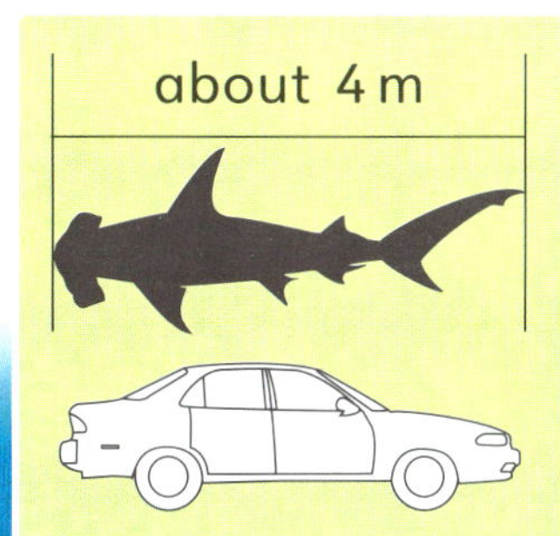

The hammerhead shark has an odd-shaped head. The hammer shape helps the shark to make sharp turns in the water.

Koi

Koi can live to be 100 years old. They were first bred in Japan for their beauty. Now they are kept in garden ponds everywhere.

Lantern Fish

The lantern fish has lights on its head and body. It lives in the darkest parts of the ocean. The lantern fish uses its lights to tempt little fish closer so it can eat them.

Lion Fish

The lion fish has fins that contain poison. The fins quickly kill a much bigger fish.

fins

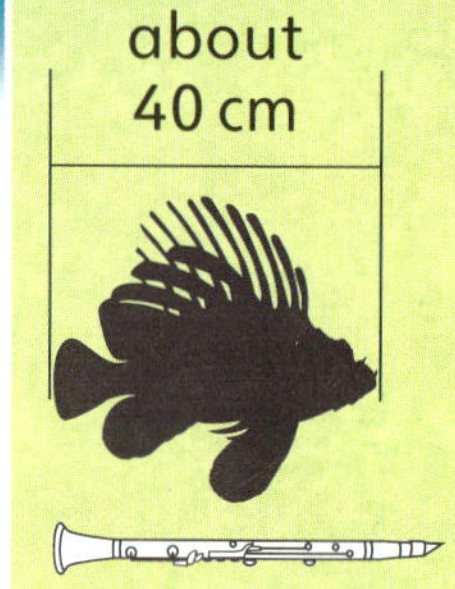

Manta Ray

The manta ray has fins that look like wings. Although it is big and looks fierce, the manta ray is gentle and graceful.

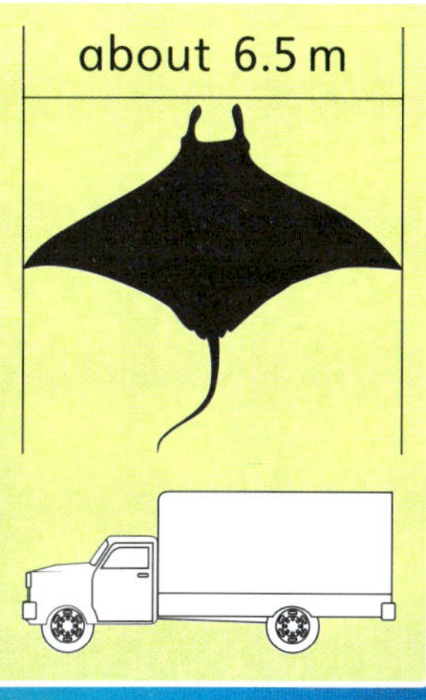

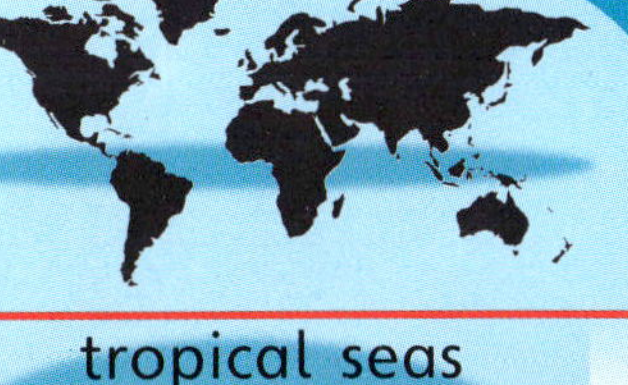

tropical seas

Mudskipper

Mudskippers can walk on land. They use their fins as crutches to skip across the muddy shore. Mudskippers eat insects living in the mud.

Ocean Sunfish

Ocean sunfish float at the top of the ocean where it is sunny.

Ocean sunfish can lay more eggs than any other fish. One fish can lay 300 000 eggs at a time. Each egg is smaller than the head of a pin.

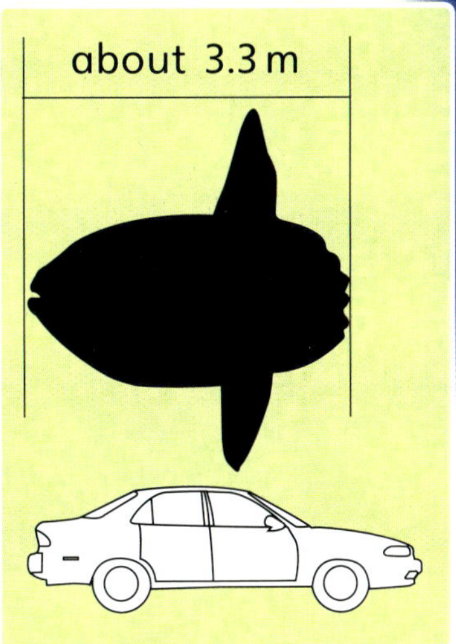

about 3.3 m

Piranha

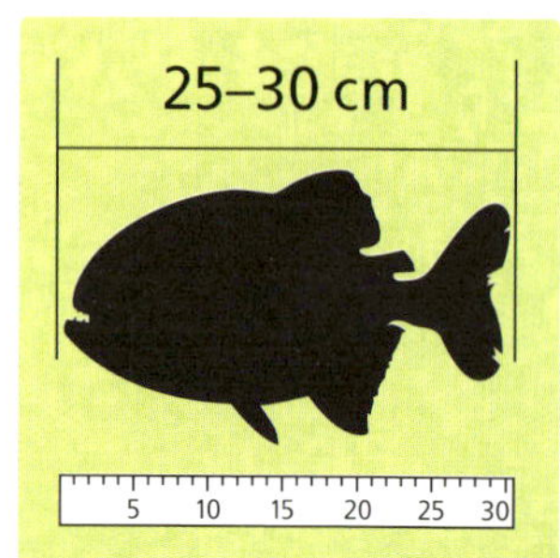

Piranhas have teeth like **razors**. They eat animals that live in rivers. Piranhas also eat fruit and seeds.

razor-sharp teeth

Amazon Basin

Porcupine Fish

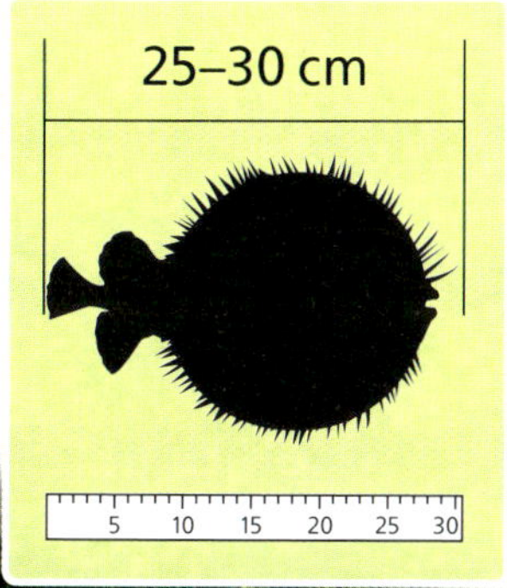
25–30 cm
5
10
15
20
25
30

The porcupine fish blows up like a balloon to look big and scary.

It is covered with poisonous spines. The spines protect the porcupine fish from bigger fish.

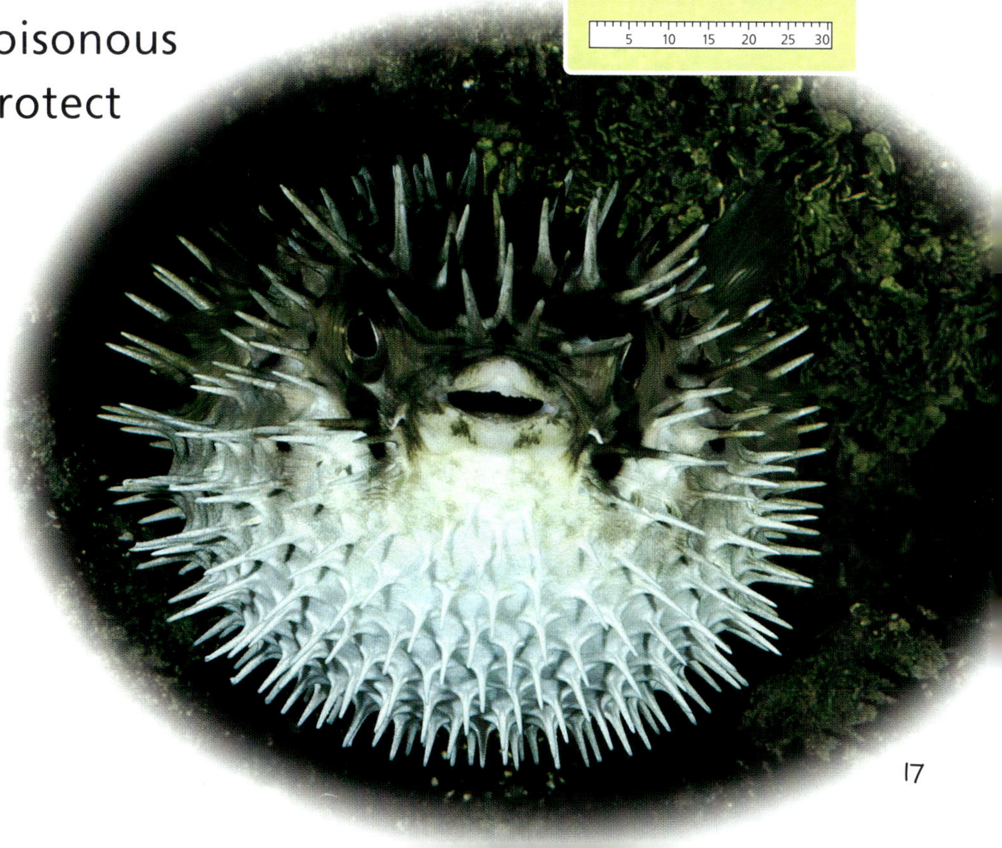

warm seas

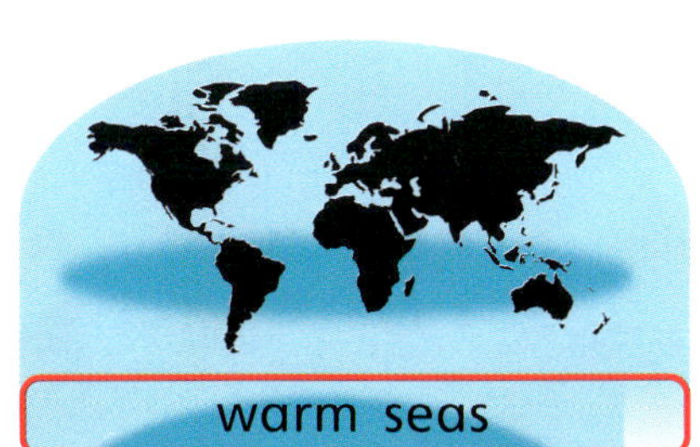

Russian Sturgeon

The Russian sturgeon's eggs are very valuable. People like to eat the eggs, which are called caviar. One fish can produce 23 kilograms of eggs.

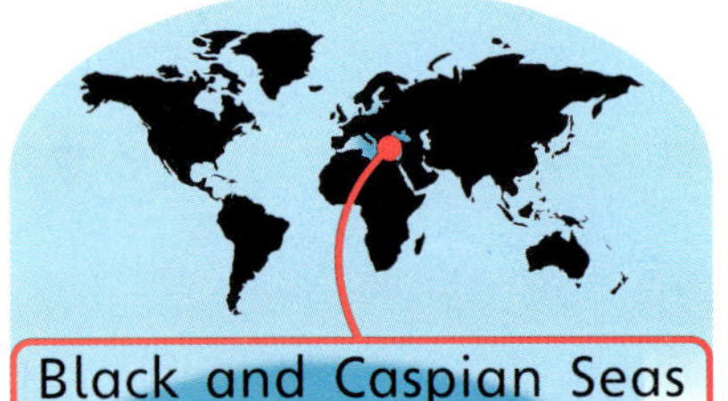

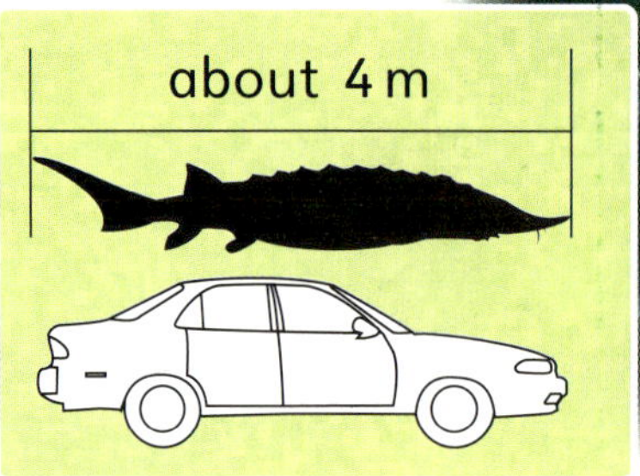

about 4 m

Sailfish

A sailfish can swim as fast as a cheetah can run. It is the fastest fish in the ocean.

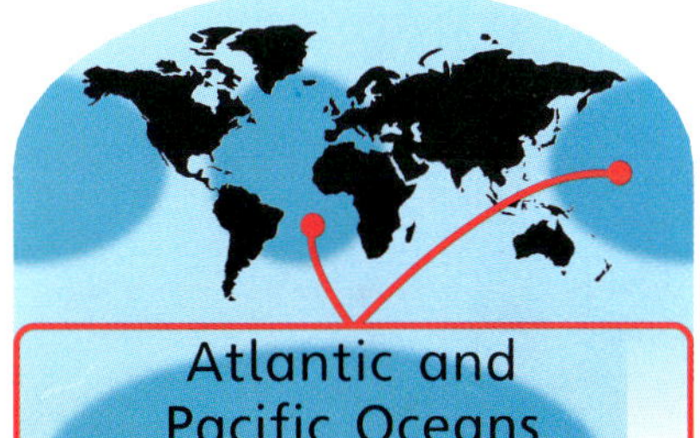

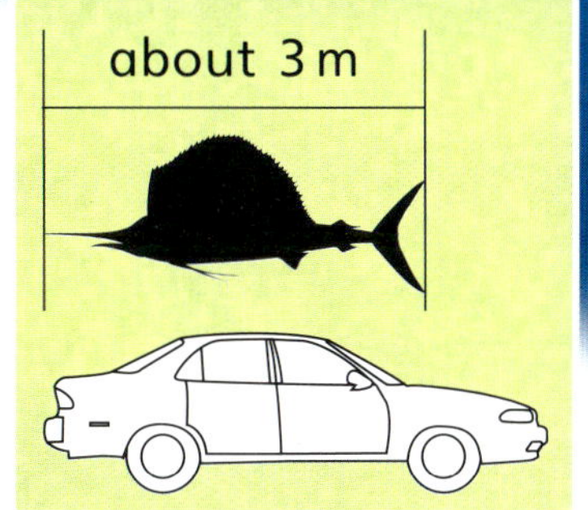

Salmon

Salmon are strong enough to swim upstream against rushing water and jump up waterfalls. Adult salmon live in the ocean, but they swim back up rivers to lay their eggs in the place where they were born.

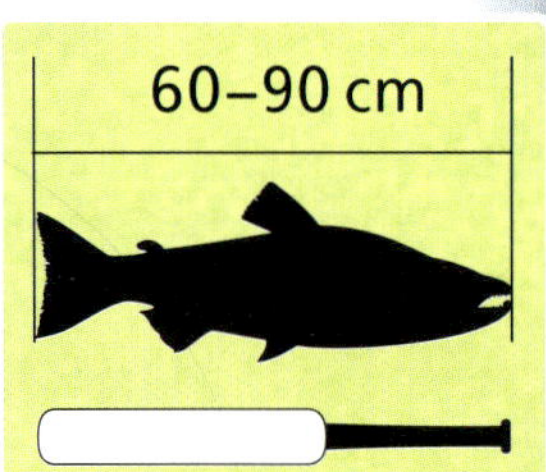

Trumpet Fish

The tube-shaped trumpet fish stands on its head, waiting to suck up **prey** that comes too close. The trumpet fish looks just like the coral that it hides in.

coral

trumpet fish

Whale Shark

The world's biggest fish has very small teeth. The whale shark has 300 rows of tiny teeth, which are useless for catching food. Instead, the whale shark uses gills like a net to scoop up **plankton**.

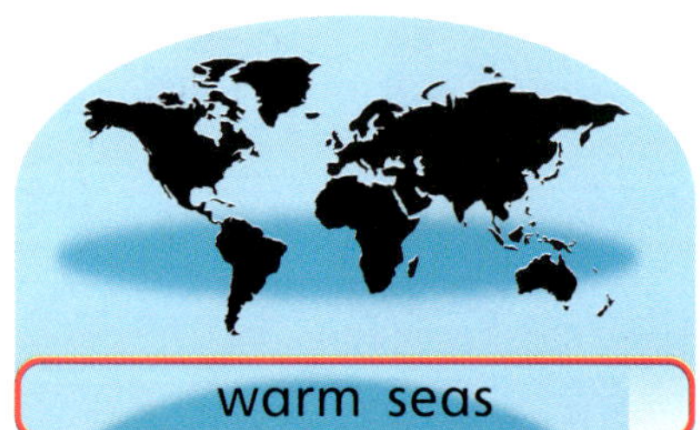

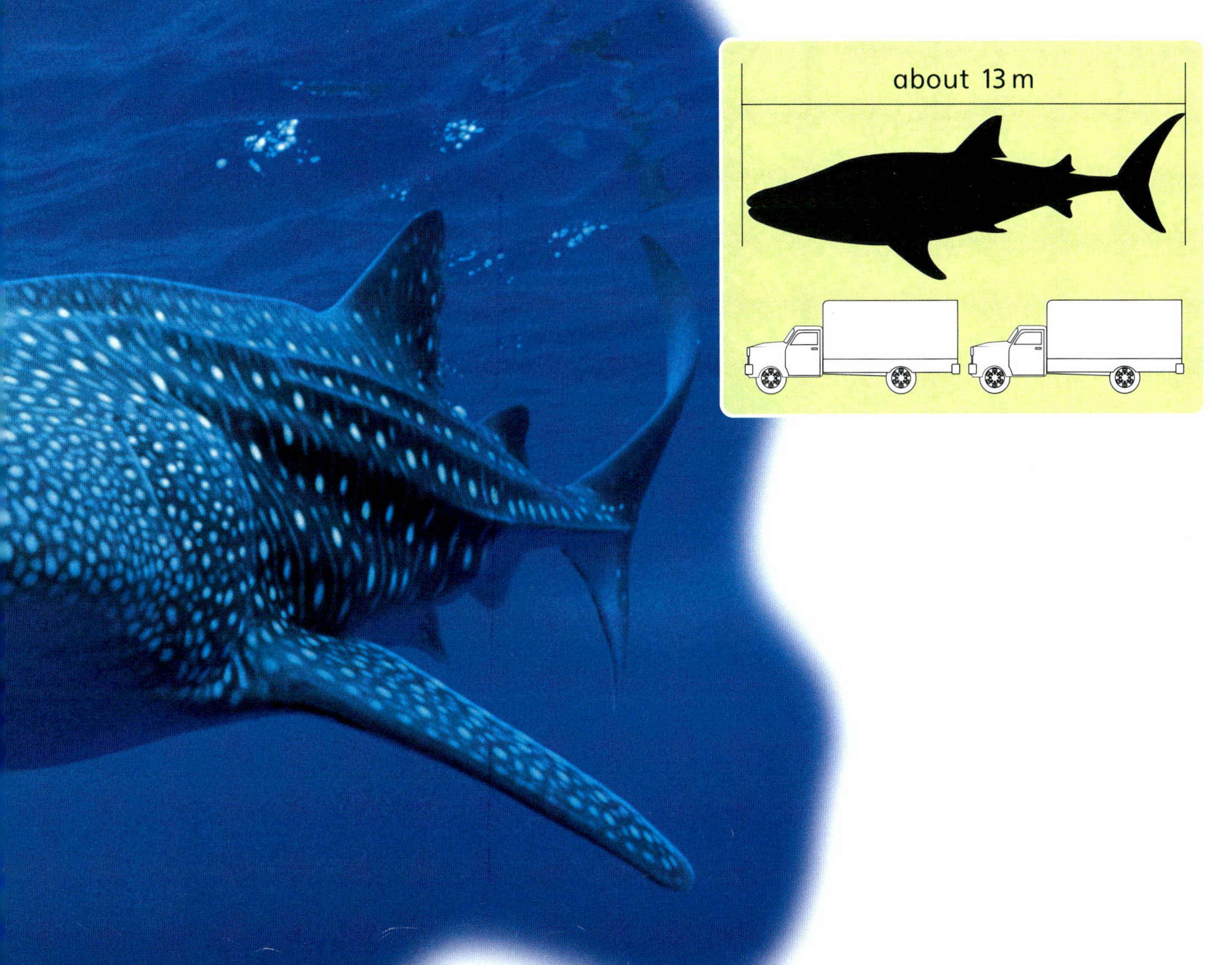

about 13 m

Glossary

plankton	tiny plants and animals that float in water
predator	an animal that hunts prey for food
prey	an animal hunted for food
razor	a very sharp cutting tool
sea anemone	a brightly coloured animal that looks like a flower, with tentacles around its mouth
tentacles	long flexible arms